GRAPHIC HISTORY

Paul Revere's RIDE

by Xavier Niz

illustrated by Brian Bascle

Consultant:

Wayne Bodle, Assistant Professor of History

Indiana University of Pennsylvania

Indiana, Pennsylvania

D1310912

Capstone press

Mankato, Minnesota

Graphic Library is published by Capstone Press,
151 Good Counsel Drive, P.O. Box 669, Mankato, Minnesota 56002.
www.capstonepress.com

Printed in the United States of America in Stevens Point, Wisconsin.
052013
007387R

Library of Congress Cataloging-in-Publication Data
Niz, Xavier.
    Paul Revere's ride / by Xavier Niz ; illustrated by Brian Bascle.
    p. cm.—(Graphic library. Graphic history)
    Includes bibliographical references and index.
    ISBN-13: 978-0-7368-4965-4 (hardcover)
    ISBN-10: 0-7368-4965-3 (hardcover)
    ISBN-13: 978-0-7368-6209-7 (softcover pbk.)
    ISBN-10: 0-7368-6209-9 (softcover pbk.)
    1. Revere, Paul, 1735–1818—Juvenile literature. 2. Massachusetts—History—Revolution,
1775–1783—Juvenile literature. 3. Lexington, Battle of, Lexington, Mass., 1775—Juvenile
literature. 4. Concord, Battle of, Concord, Mass., 1775—Juvenile literature. 5. Statesmen—
Massachusetts—Biography—Juvenile literature. 6. Massachusetts—Biography—Juvenile
literature. I. Bascle, Brian, ill. II. Title. III. Series.
F69.R43N59 2006
973.3'311'092—dc22   200500652

Summary: In graphic novel format, tells the story of Paul Revere's ride to Lexington in
April 1775 to warn colonists of approaching British troops.

Art and Editorial Direction
Jason Knudson and Blake A. Hoena

Designers
Bob Lentz and Juliette Peters

Editor
Donald Lemke

Editor's note: Direct quotations from primary sources are indicated by a yellow background.

Direct quotations appear on the following pages:
Pages 12, 20, from *Paul Revere's Three Accounts of His Famous Ride* by Paul Revere (Boston:
    Massachusetts Historical Society, 1976).
Pages 14, 19, from *Paul Revere's Ride* by David Hackett Fischer (New York: Oxford
    University Press, 1994).

TABLE of CONTENTS

Chapter 1

The GENERAL'S PLAN

During the 1760s, Great Britain controlled 13 colonies in North America. Some colonists were tired of British rule. They didn't want to pay taxes without having a say in the government. These people became known as Whigs.

In Boston, Massachusetts, a young silversmith named Paul Revere joined other Whigs in protests.

No taxation without representation!

He's right!

The protests forced Great Britain to stop taxing all goods except tea. But the tax on the colonists' favorite drink sparked even more protests. On December 16, 1773, Revere stood guard as colonists dumped British tea into Boston Harbor.

British leaders were furious over what became known as the Boston Tea Party. They passed a set of harsh laws and made British General Thomas Gage the governor of Massachusetts.

We will restore order to these unruly colonies!

Dr. Warren had a friend in the British camp.

You must ride to Lexington and warn Hancock and Adams.

General Gage plans to arrest Adams and Hancock in Lexington and then march to Concord.

We can't let Gage succeed!

Oh no! I need to get this news to Paul.

Of course! I will leave at once.

The RACE to LEXINGTON

On the night of April 18, 1775, Revere rushed to the docks along the Charles River. To deliver his message, Revere had to cross the river to Charlestown.

Have you heard the news?

Yes. The boat is ready.

To avoid more British soldiers, Revere decided to travel along Mystic Road. It was a longer route to Lexington but safer. On his way, he alerted people to what was happening.

Be warned!

The Regulars are coming this way.

I'll get the men ready for a fight!

Chapter 3

ON to CONCORD

Before leaving Lexington, Paul Revere thought up a plan. The three riders would take turns stopping at every house on their way to Concord.

The British are coming!

Be warned! The Regulars are on their way to capture the stored weapons at Concord.

Spread the news!

The British commander questioned Revere.

What's your name?

Paul Revere.

So you're the one warning the colonists of our plan?

Yes! And now, I must warn you, Major.

There are 500 militiamen gathering in Lexington.

You will not succeed!

We'll see about that, Revere.

Chapter 4
The Start of a Revolution

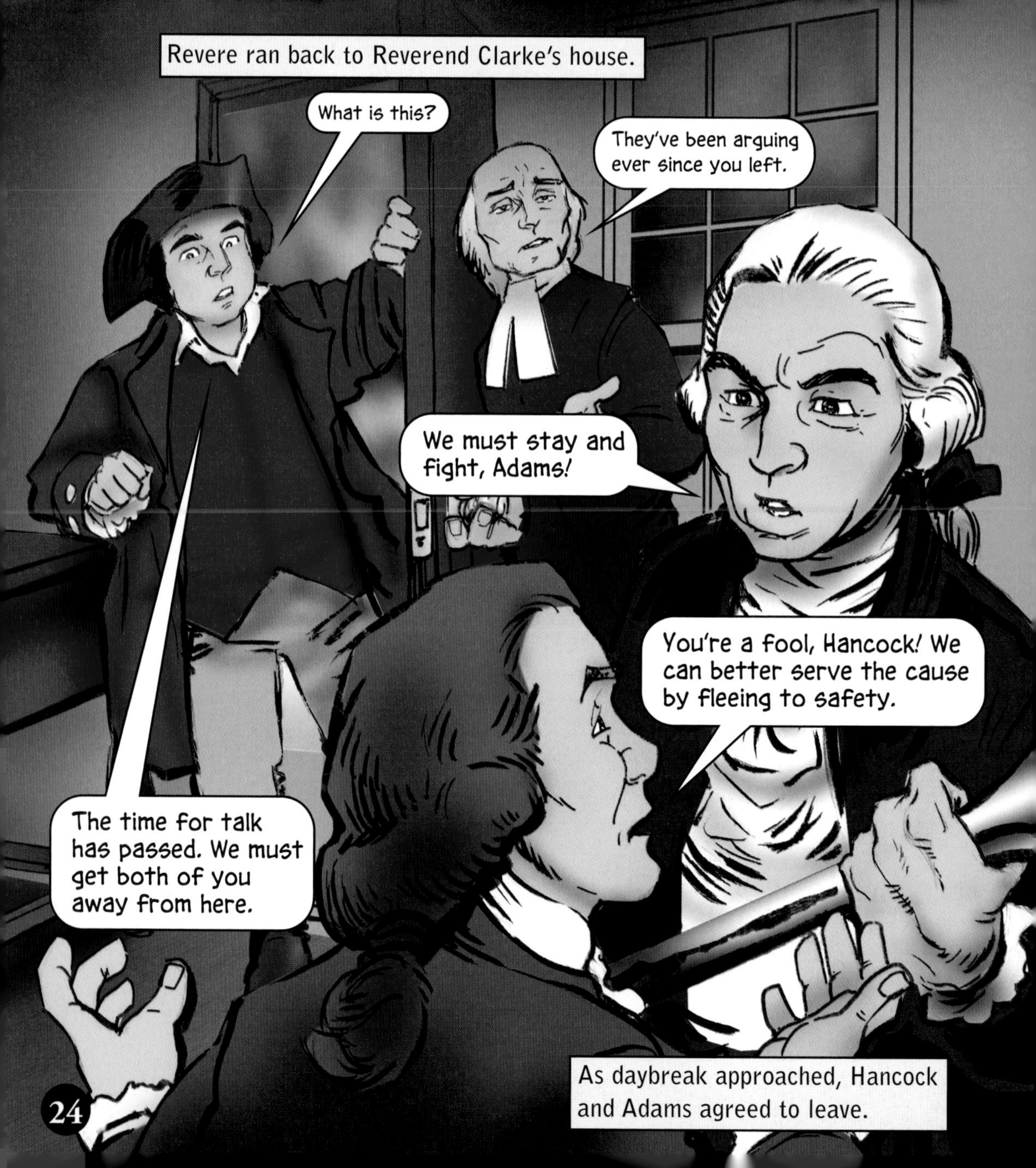

Now that Hancock and Adams were gone, Revere thought he could finally rest.

Suddenly, there was a knock at the door.

Hancock left a trunk filled with important papers at Buckman Tavern!

It's too heavy to carry by myself. Will you help me?

Of course, let us go rescue that trunk of yours.

Revere and John Lowell rushed to the tavern. Inside, the local militia greeted them.

The trunk's in the attic, Paul.

First, let me ask these men about the shots I heard earlier.

Lowell and Revere got the trunk from the tavern and escaped into the nearby woods.

Did you hear that?

Yes. I wonder who fired the first shot?

The men of Lexington didn't stand a chance against the British. But Hancock and Adams had escaped. News of the British plan had reached the Whigs in Concord. By the time the British got there, most of the weapons had been moved. The British were driven out of Concord and forced back to Boston.

By the end of the day, the American Revolution had begun.

More about

PAUL REVERE'S RIDE

* Paul Revere was born in December 1734. His father, Apollos Rivoire, came to America from France. After marrying an American colonist named Deborah Hichborn, Rivoire changed his name to Revere.

* Paul Revere wasn't just a silversmith. He also made things with gold and copper. He even made false teeth and worked as a dentist. Eventually, Revere launched a successful business making copper sheeting.

* Some people believe the horse Paul Revere borrowed from Larkin was named Brown Beauty. After the British took the horse, neither Revere nor Larkin ever saw the horse again.

* Only 70 militiamen were gathered in Lexington when British troops arrived. They fought against 238 British soldiers. When the battle was over, eight members of the colonial militia were dead. Ten more were wounded. Only one British soldier had been hurt.

* To this day, no one knows who fired the first shot at the Battle of Lexington.

About 700 British troops set out from Boston for Concord. By the time they returned to Boston, more than 250 of the soldiers had been wounded or killed.

Paul Revere died of natural causes on May 10, 1818. He was 83 years old.

The heroic deeds of Paul Revere were largely forgotten after the Revolutionary War. In 1860, Henry Wadsworth Longfellow wrote the poem "Paul Revere's Midnight Ride." Soon, the poem and the story of Paul Revere became famous.

Today, people from all over the world visit Paul Revere's house. It is the oldest building in downtown Boston and a reminder of a great American.

GLOSSARY

militia (muh-LISH-uh)—a group of volunteer citizens who are trained to fight battles

Redcoat (RED-koht)—a British soldier during the Revolutionary War; the name came from the bright red coats the soldiers wore.

representative (rep-ri-ZEN-tuh-tiv)—a person elected to serve in a government

silversmith (SIL-vur-smith)—a person who makes items out of silver, such as spoons, jewelry, and teapots

tax (TAKS)—money collected from a country's citizens to help pay for running the government

INTERNET SITES

FactHound offers a safe, fun way to find Internet sites related to this book. All of the sites on FactHound have been researched by our staff.

Here's how:

1. *Visit www.facthound.com*
2. Type in this special code **0736849653** for age-appropriate sites. Or enter a search word related to this book for a more general search.
3. Click on the **Fetch It** button.

FactHound will fetch the best sites for you!

READ MORE

Burke, Rick. *Paul Revere.* American Lives. Chicago: Heinemann Library, 2003.

Golden, Nancy. *The British Are Coming!: The Midnight Ride of Paul Revere.* Great Moments in American History. New York: Rosen Central Primary Source, 2004.

Raatma, Lucia. *The Battles of Lexington and Concord.* We the People. Minneapolis: Compass Point Books, 2004.

Rosen, Daniel. *Independence Now: The American Revolution, 1763–1783.* Crossroads America. Washington, DC: National Geographic, 2004.

BIBLIOGRAPHY

Fischer, David Hackett. *Paul Revere's Ride.* New York: Oxford University Press, 1994.

Revere, Paul. *Paul Revere's Three Accounts of His Famous Ride.* Boston: Massachusetts Historical Society, 1976.

Triber, Jayne E. *A True Republican: The Life of Paul Revere.* Amherst: University of Massachusetts Press, 1998.

Index